Bigfoot

These and other titles are included in the Exploring the Unknown series:

Bigfoot

by Julie S. Bach

Lucent Books, P.O. Box 289011, San Diego, CA 92198-9011

Library of Congress Cataloging-in-Publication Data
Bach, Julie S., 1963-
    Bigfoot / by Julie S. Bach.
        p. cm.—(Exploring the unknown)
    Includes bibliographical references (p.   ) and index.
    ISBN 1-56006-160-X (acid-free paper)
    1. Sasquatch—Juvenile literature.   [1. Sasquatch.]
    I. Title.   II. Series: Exploring the unknown (San Diego, Calif.)
    QL89.2.S2B32   1995
    001.9'44—dc20   94-11570
                                                                            CIP
                                                                             AC

CONTENTS

For Ryan

The Beast in the Woods

On May 24, 1988, four friends were camping in Waterton Lakes National Park in Alberta, Canada. The two men and two women stayed up late at their campsite, talking and playing cards until after midnight. Finally they were ready for bed. Then something happened that they will never forget.

Steve and Sarah (newspapers did not report the couples' last names) walked down a path leading from the campsite. They were going to brush their teeth. Sarah heard a noise and stopped in alarm. Steve heard nothing and kept walking. He had never been afraid of the forest's night noises. But suddenly he realized that something very large was standing on the path in front of him.

"It's a bear!" Sarah yelled. She ran back to the campsite. George and Margaret heard Sarah yell. They panicked and ran for the cars. In the confusion, George got in one car and Margaret got in another. Sarah rushed into George's car. But where was Steve? The three friends scanned the woods, searching for Steve. Then they saw him.

He was slowly backing down the trail away from the shape he had seen. It had disappeared, but Steve thought he heard something in the trees beside him. He was no longer sure where the creature had gone.

Finally, he reached the campsite. He raced for the cars and jumped in with Margaret.

"Turn on your headlights!" George yelled from the other car. Margaret did. The lights from the two cars lit up a large section of trees.

Within minutes, the frightened couples saw an enormous hairy beast walk into the pool of light. It was eight feet tall and covered with black hair. It had very long arms. It walked across the area lit by the headlights, then disappeared into the woods.

The next morning the four campers reported their story to the park warden. It may have sounded like a tall tale, but they insisted they were telling the truth. Later, reporters interviewed the four friends separately. Their stories were identical, and many people believed them.

If their story was true, what was the huge creature they had seen in their headlights? Was it an animal? Was it a big, furry human being? Or was it something much more mysterious?

A Huge, Hairy Monster

The four friends were not the first people to see such a creature. For hundreds of years, many people have claimed that a huge, hairy monster lives in remote areas of the United States and Canada. They call this being Bigfoot.

People say Bigfoot is eight feet tall. It can weigh up to a thousand pounds, and it can lift things a person could never even budge. People who have seen Bigfoot say it is covered with hair, usually black or brown. Its arms are long, and it has a strong odor. Some people say it makes a high-pitched whistling sound.

Another name for Bigfoot is Sasquatch. And, people say, there are more than one of them. One man even claims to have seen a family of Sasquatches.

Few people have seen an actual Bigfoot. But many people have seen its tracks. Some have even made plaster casts of Bigfoot's footprints. Its footprints can be up to twenty-four inches long and eight inches wide.

In spite of the many sightings, prints, and other evidence, many people doubt that Bigfoot exists. They think people are telling stories just for the fun of it. There must be a simple explanation, they say, even for the mysteriously huge footprints.

Other people see no reason to doubt that it is real. John Napier is an author and former director of primate biology at the Smithsonian Institution. He says, "I am convinced the Sasquatch exists." Whatever their beliefs, many scientists and adventurers would like to solve the mystery once and for all.

CHAPTER 1

A Mysterious Legend

Legends of Bigfoot go back hundreds of years. The first tales of a humanlike monster roaming the woods were told by the native peoples of North America. Each tribe gave the creature a different name.

The Salish Indians of southwest British Columbia, Canada, were the first to call it Sasquatch, which means "wild man of the woods." Their name for Bigfoot is still popular today. The Huppa tribe of northern California calls it Oh-mah-'ah, often shortened to Omah. The Kwakiutl in British Columbia call it Tsonokwa. The Cree in Manitoba, Canada, call it Weeketow. In Florida, the Seminoles call it by a name that means the Sand Man.

The Clallam and Quinault tribes in northern California tell of creatures called Seeahtiks. The Seeahtiks, they say, are half human and half monster. They are seven to eight-feet tall and can make themselves invisible. The Seeahtiks may be another version of Bigfoot.

The Karok Indians, also of northern California, have a legend about "upslope persons." According to the legend, the upslopes are big, hairy, and strong but not very smart. They live far up in the mountains. The Karoks are wary of upslopes. In one folktale, an upslope person captures and eats the children of Long-billed Dowitcher. (A dowitcher is a wading bird like a sandpiper.) Long-billed Dowitcher kills the upslope and restores his children to life.

Not all stories show Bigfoot as bad. The Yurok tribe has a legend about a young woman who disappeared from her village near what is now Bluff Creek, in California. When she returned, she brought with her a newborn baby and five baskets of valuable shells. According to the legend, she had married a giant. The Yuroks say she married Bigfoot.

Early Written Accounts

The first written account of a mysterious creature in the North American wilderness comes from a Canadian geographer named David Thompson. From 1792 to 1812, he traveled large sections of western Canada and the northwestern United States, making maps.

One day, in 1811, Thompson was traveling in Alberta, Canada, near what is now Jasper National Park. He came upon a set of tracks. They were fourteen inches long and eight inches wide. He was sure they were not the tracks of a bear—or any other animal he had seen before. But what were they? Thompson carefully recorded this unexplained incident in his writings.

A pioneer missionary to the Spokane Indians in what is now the state of Washington also wrote of strange creatures. These were described to him by the Indians. The missionary, Elkanah Walker, wrote in 1840: "[Spokanes] believe in a race

The Spokane Indians of Washington called the Bigfoot man stealers. They believed that, deep in the night, Bigfoot stole their sleeping children and took fish from their nets.

of giants which inhabit a certain mountain off to the west of us." He was probably referring to Mount Rainier, Mount St. Helens, or another of the Cascade Mountains.

This race of giants, he wrote, lived on the snow-covered top of the mountain. They were

> men stealers. They come to people's lodges at night when the people are asleep and put them under their skins [skin clothing] and [take them] to their place of abode [home] without even waking [them]. Their track is a foot and a half long. . . . They steal salmon from Indian nets and eat them raw, as bears do. . . . If the people are awake, they always know when they are coming very near, by their strong smell, which is most intolerable. It is not uncommon for them to come in the night and give three whistles and then the stones will begin to hit their houses.

Walker thought the Spokanes were superstitious. He thought they imagined the giants. He never saw the creatures himself. But his interesting description provides many details that are echoed by people who report seeing Bigfoot today.

A President's Tale

Theodore Roosevelt was an adventurer as well as a president. On one of his trips to the northwestern United States before he became president, he heard an interesting and frightening story. He reported it in his 1892 book *The Wilderness Hunter*. The story was about two trappers. One of them, a Mr. Baumann, survived to tell the tale to Roosevelt. The other did not.

Back in the 1860s, Baumann said, he and his friend were trapping beaver in the mountains of Idaho. They knew that a year before, a trapper's body had been found in the same area they were camping in. The body was badly damaged and partially eaten by some kind of animal. Huge footprints, similar to those of a human, were found near the body. The animal that had killed the man was never found.

Even knowing this story, Baumann and his friend trekked deep into the mountain wilderness, camping and trapping. One evening, they returned from their day's work, setting and checking traps, only to find their campsite completely torn apart. They assumed a bear had wandered in and, attracted by food smells, had ripped up the site and many of their supplies. They found large tracks that didn't look like a bear's. "That bear has been walking on two legs," Baumann's friend said.

Baumann laughed, and the two friends cleaned things up, fixed a meal, and went to bed.

That night around midnight, they were awakened by loud noises and by a terrible, wild-beast smell. Baumann saw a huge shape looming over the entrance to their lean-to. He grabbed his rifle and fired, but he missed. The creature smashed through the underbrush, running away from the rifle and the men.

The next night, the two trappers kept a fire going all night, and they took turns standing guard. Repeatedly, they heard a heavy creature thrashing around in the woods nearby. The next morning, they decided to move their camp.

Baumann's friend stayed at the camp to pack things up, while Baumann went off to pick up their traps. He was gone longer than he had expected. Some of the traps had beaver in them, and he needed to skin them right away so they wouldn't spoil. When he got back to camp, he found his friend dead. Teddy Roosevelt wrote:

> The horrified trapper found that the body was still warm, but that the neck was broken, while there were four great fang marks in the throat.
>
> The footprints of the unknown beast, printed deep in the soft soil, told the whole story. . . . It had not eaten the body, but apparently had romped and gambolled around it in uncouth and ferocious glee, occasionally rolling it over and over; and had then fled back into the soundless depths of the woods.

Baumann was shocked and terrified. He left everything except his rifle and took off down the trail until he came to a place where the men had left their ponies. He hopped on a horse and rode at top speed until he had reached safety.

Baumann never knew for sure what had killed his friend, but many think it was a Bigfoot.

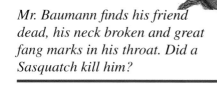

Mr. Baumann finds his friend dead, his neck broken and great fang marks in his throat. Did a Sasquatch kill him?

Is Bigfoot a Joke?

In May 1977, Dennis Gates, a Bigfoot researcher, got the news that a Bigfoot had been sighted in northern Washington—by six witnesses. Gates sped to the scene, about eighty miles from his home. There he met two other Bigfoot researchers, John Green and René Dahinden. They talked with Pat Lindquist, the Pacific Stage Lines bus driver who had seen Bigfoot. Lindquist had been driving down the highway when suddenly a large, hairy creature had stepped out of the woods and walked across the road. Lindquist braked and shouted to his passengers, "Look at the Sasquatch!"

Everyone saw the creature. Lindquist hopped out of the bus and ran across the road after it. He smelled an overpowering stench and saw several tracks. Then he spied Bigfoot.

Lindquist ran back to his bus; Bigfoot ran deeper into the woods. Lindquist continued to the next town and reported his sighting to the authorities.

Three experts arrived to investigate. They took many measurements and photographs of the tracks. They also made plaster casts. They were impressed with the quality of the footprints. Those and the eyewitness accounts seemed to assure the truth of the story. Headlines on newspapers around the country announced that Bigfoot had been seen.

Then the photographs were developed. The photos showed something the eyes couldn't see. The prints were not made by natural feet. They were fakes. The experts were disappointed and the public was upset. Soon after the hoax was made public, a young man called a radio station and told how he and his friends had pulled off their hoax. They had taken three weeks to carefully plan it. They used a gorilla suit, walkie-talkies to coordinate everything, and fake footprints. They even planted one of their group on the bus just in case no one noticed the "Bigfoot" walking across the road. Don Ticehurst, one of the pranksters, said, "It was just a good practical joke. We thought it might fool a few people. We meant no harm."

An Unbelievable Story

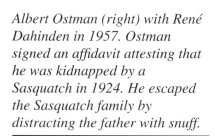

Albert Ostman (right) with René Dahinden in 1957. Ostman signed an affidavit attesting that he was kidnapped by a Sasquatch in 1924. He escaped the Sasquatch family by distracting the father with snuff.

Reports of Bigfoot sightings were not common around the turn of the century. If people did see mysterious tracks or even encounter a Sasquatch, they usually kept their stories to themselves. That is exactly what Albert Ostman did after he was kidnapped by a family of Bigfoots!

In 1924, Ostman decided to take a vacation and go prospecting for gold. One night, he was asleep on the ground, rolled up in his sleeping bag. Suddenly, he felt himself being picked up and carried away. Whatever was carrying Ostman must have been very strong. It carried Ostman, his rifle, and his knapsack, all still in the sleeping bag. The creature carried Ostman for what he guessed was about three hours.

Finally, the beast dropped Ostman to the ground. It was still dark, but as dawn came and the sky got lighter, he could see that he was in a valley surrounded by mountains. He could also see that four large

Sasquatches were standing around him.

Ostman said the Sasquatches never harmed him. They appeared to be a family—a father, mother, and two children. Ostman described the father as eight feet tall, with huge arms and legs, large forearms, and large hands. All four creatures were covered with hair except for their feet, the palms of their hands, their noses, and their eyelids. Their feet were padded underneath like a dog's. Yet, said Ostman, they seemed more human than animal.

Ostman was with the Bigfoot family almost a week. He eventually escaped by distracting them with his snuff, or smoke-less tobacco. The creatures ate the tobacco and screamed in surprise and pain. Ostman grabbed his rifle and ran for the woods, firing once to scare them off.

Ostman told no one about his week with the Sasquatches. He was afraid people would laugh at him. Then, in 1957, he read several newspaper accounts about sightings of Bigfoot. He told his story and hoped people would believe him. But many people wondered. Could Ostman be telling the truth?

By the late 1950s, many people had reported sightings of large, mysterious creatures. The notion of a wild being lurking in the woods was becoming a popular idea. Still, not much was known about the Sasquatch. It would take a few more stories and a new name before the legend of Bigfoot would become as popular as it is today.

In 1958, Gerald ("Jerry") Crew worked for a road construction company in northwestern California. They were working in terrain so rugged it had been surveyed only from the air. Crew drove a bulldozer. His job was to clear the trees and underbrush so roads could be built through the woods.

During the week, Crew and the other workers lived at a camp in the mountains. On the weekends, they drove home to their families. On Friday, August 24, Crew was the last to leave for home. He ran the bulldozer back and forth over fresh, soft earth. Then he drove it down the mountain to his pickup truck. The only tracks he left on the ground were those of the tractor and his own boots.

Bulldozer operator Jerry Crew and his coworkers found signs of a Bigfoot near their work site.

Strange Footprints

On the following Monday morning, Crew returned to work. With a tap on his horn, he greeted the job supervisor standing in the doorway of the shack that served as an office. The supervisor waved back. Crew drove his truck on up the mountain and parked near his bulldozer. He got out of his truck and stood for a moment enjoying the morning stillness of the forest. Then he put on his hard hat.

As Crew strolled toward his machine, he noticed several large footprints in the dirt. Bear tracks, he thought. He climbed aboard the high seat of his bulldozer. But when he looked down, he saw a whole line of footprints approaching the bulldozer. They circled it, then continued down the edge of the raw roadway. These tracks were larger than any he had ever seen.

Crew jumped to the ground and stared at the footprints. They were huge. His own tracks looked like a child's beside them. He tried to walk in the tracks, but they were too far apart. Whatever had made them had a very long stride.

This must be a joke, Crew thought. Maybe some of his friends had made the tracks to play a trick on him. But who would bother to come all the way up the mountain after a long week of work just for a joke? Besides, Crew could see only two sets of tracks: his own and the big-footed ones.

Jerry Crew began to feel uneasy. He hopped in his truck and drove down the mountain to tell his supervisor, Wilbur Wallace.

Other Mysterious Incidents

Wallace had no idea what to make of the tracks, but he remembered two other mysterious incidents. The summer before, his workers had found a fifty-five-gallon metal drum at the bottom of a hill. They were sure it had been picked up and *thrown* over the side of a drop-off. And just two weeks ago, a worker had found a seven-hundred-pound tire at the bottom of a ravine. It had apparently been pushed or thrown there.

Some of the workers laughed at Crew's story, but others were frightened. Wallace told them not to worry.

On October 1, Crew saw footprints again. This time he filled one of them with plaster and made a cast of it. Because the footprints were so big, he named the mysterious creature Bigfoot.

A northern California newspaper, *The Humboldt Times*, photographed Crew and his cast. The photograph appeared in newspapers across the country. The name stuck. Bigfoot had become part of American folklore.

CHAPTER 2

Searching for Bigfoot

If Bigfoot is real, a cryptozoologist will probably be the one to prove it. Cryptozoology is the study of unseen animals. The name comes from the Greek word *kryptos* for "hidden" and the word *zoology*, meaning the science of animal life. The term was coined by Bernard Heuvelmans, a Belgian zoologist. He is recognized as the founder of cryptozoology.

Many people are skeptical of cryptozoologists because the animals they search for seem imaginary. Besides Bigfoot, these scientists are looking for the Loch Ness Monster in Scotland; the onza, a large catlike creature, in Mexico; and the Mokele-Mbembe, a swamp creature, in Africa. One of the animals they seek, the yeti, may be related to Bigfoot. But no one has been able to prove that any of these creatures exist.

The skeptics have not kept people from looking for Bigfoot. Cryptozoologists, adventurers, and other curious people have spent time and money tracking the Sasquatch.

A Famous Mountain Climber

Halfway around the world from where Jerry Crew discovered the mysterious footprints, the people of Nepal tell stories of the yeti, a half-human, half-animal creature that is rarely seen. It lives high up in the Himalaya Mountains. People have seen its huge footprints in the snow.

In some accounts, the yeti is six feet tall. In others, it is fifteen feet tall! It is said to have a terrible smell, and people call it the Abominable Snowman. Many people think it is a relative of Bigfoot.

The native people of Nepal stay away from the yeti. But foreign visitors have wondered about this mysterious creature. One curious person was Sir Edmund Hillary, a mountaineer from New Zealand. He and his Sherpa guide, Tenzing Norkay of Tibet, became famous by being the first people to climb to the top of Mount Everest in 1953.

Stories of the yeti fascinated Hillary. On one of his expeditions in the Himalayas, he decided to look for proof that the yeti exists.

The famous mountaineer was well prepared to find a yeti. He brought cameras to take photographs and plaster to make casts of any footprints his team found. He also brought tranquilizing guns. If they were lucky enough to run into a yeti, Hillary wanted to stun the creature and examine it. He would not kill it, because the religion of Nepal, where he was looking, forbids killing animals.

Many people were excited about Hillary's expedition. They hoped he would find a yeti.

Near one village, the expedition found large footprints in the snow. The team took photographs and made plaster casts to be examined later.

(Bottom) Sardar Tenzing Norkay (right) and Edmund P. Hillary in the clothes they wore to climb Mount Everest. (Top) Hillary with the mysterious scalp given to him by villagers who claimed it was the scalp of a yeti.

The Mysterious Scalp

Then, in the village of Khumjung, Hillary was shown a scalp. The villagers said it was the scalp of a yeti. Hillary asked if he could take the scalp to be examined. He promised to return it safely.

Could this be the proof everyone was looking for? The members of the expedition were hopeful. But scientists in Chicago said the scalp was that of a serow, a wild goat antelope. Scientists in Paris said it was a bear.

John Napier, an author and anthropologist, believes Hillary was given a copy of the scalp, not the real scalp itself. He thinks the scientists in Chicago and Paris were fooled by the copy.

What about the footprints? Desmond Doig is a journalist and mountaineer who was on the expedition. He believed that the prints must have been made by a Tibetan blue bear. Blue bears, he explained, sometimes walk on their hind legs.

Napier believes Desmond Doig is wrong. Blue bears do not *walk* on their hind legs, he says. "They may briefly stand upright on two legs, but they certainly never walk on them." Napier believes the tracks were made by a yeti.

George Schaller is an ethologist, a person who studies human and animal behavior. He is convinced that "an animal unknown to science" lives in the Himalayas.

A Patient Listener

Hillary's expedition turned out to be a disappointment. But that did not stop others from searching for unknown creatures.

René Dahinden has been looking for Bigfoot for forty years. His search started out as a hobby, something to do for fun. But it soon became his life's work.

In 1953, Dahinden was working on a farm in Canada. He heard radio reports of an expedition being formed to search for the yeti in the Himalayas. He was fascinated by the idea of such creatures.

The next year, Dahinden moved to British Columbia. He spent hours in the Vancouver public library reading accounts of Bigfoot sightings. He began to keep his own file of sightings. By 1956, he had found enough evidence to convince him that Sasquatch was real.

Dahinden began talking to people who said they had seen Bigfoot or Bigfoot's tracks. He listened carefully to their stories. He tried to judge whether the people were reliable, or whether they were simply seeking attention. Many people who had been shy about telling their stories came forward when they found such an interested listener.

People began to call Dahinden whenever a Bigfoot sighting was reported. They wanted his opinion on whether the story was real. Dahinden recorded every detail he heard. Author Don

John Napier with the cast of a foot he believes was made by a yeti. Napier believes that the footprints that Norkay and Hillary saw were authentic.

Hunter says, "The hundreds of reports that are now on record are there largely through Dahinden's persistent searching."

Still, Dahinden has never proven the existence of the Sasquatch. He has a lengthy catalog of witnesses' names, dates, and sightings, but no scientific proof. What will it take to prove that Bigfoot is real?

Scientists Join the Search

Grover Krantz, a scientist at Washington State University, has no doubt that Bigfoot exists. He has been pursuing the elusive creature since 1969. Unlike Dahinden, who examines stories of Bigfoot sightings, Krantz is more interested in the scientific truth of Bigfoot footprints. He has made and examined plaster casts of dozens of footprints.

When Krantz first began his research, he doubted that Bigfoot could exist. After seeing footprints in 1970, he changed his mind. "The bottom line is that the anatomical [bodily] characteristics I could reconstruct were things that no faker could ever come up with," he says.

Krantz is so certain Bigfoot exists that he has given the creature a scientific name. In 1986, he published a paper in which he gave Bigfoot the name *Gigantopithecus blacki*. That name already belonged to a large apelike creature known only by fossils found in China and northern India. But most scientists believe *Gigantop-*

This map shows the number of Bigfoot sightings made in North America. The red areas reveal the most sightings.

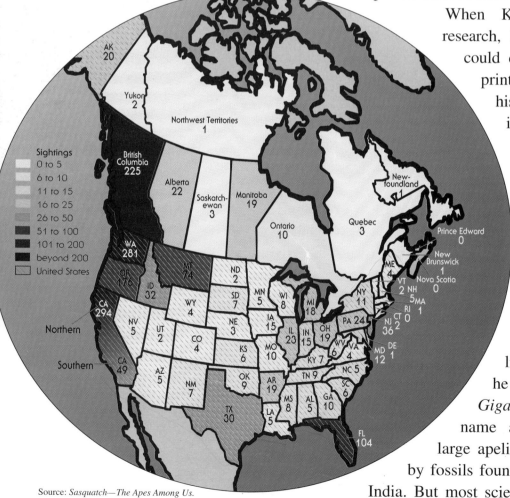

Sightings
- 0 to 5
- 6 to 10
- 11 to 15
- 16 to 25
- 26 to 50
- 51 to 100
- 101 to 200
- beyond 200
- United States

Source: *Sasquatch—The Apes Among Us.*

ithecus blacki has been extinct for half a million years. Krantz thinks a few of the creatures have survived in the Pacific Northwest.

Cryptozoologists are not surprised when other scientists are skeptical. They think most scientists are afraid to admit that Bigfoot might be real. Krantz says that established scientists fear that if Bigfoot is shown to be real, the public will lose its faith in science. Many scientists are afraid people will think, "If they have overlooked such a big creature as Bigfoot, what else have they overlooked?" But Krantz points out that new discoveries are constantly changing science. For example, it was only about twenty years ago that scientists proved that the earth's continents are not fixed in position. They are constantly and slowly drifting away from their present positions. This discovery caused a great deal of excitement and dismay among geologists. But it did not make the public lose faith in geology. In fact, Krantz says, this important discovery opened up a whole new enthusiasm for the earth sciences.

René Dahinden inspects purported Bigfoot tracks near Bluff Creek, California, in this 1967 photograph.

Scarce Research Funds

Another problem scientists have with the search for Bigfoot is money. There is only so much money to support research, and there are all kinds of fascinating and important subjects that could be studied. Scientists—and the organizations that fund them—are constantly having to decide which subjects are worth spending great amounts of money on. Many scientists believe that a lot of subjects—AIDS research and space exploration, for example—are more important than searching for a creature that may not even be real.

Bigfoot in Minnesota

In 1968, cryptozoologist Ivan Sanderson heard rumors that a mysterious human-like creature was being exhibited at the Minnesota State Fair. The creature was completely encased in ice and its features only partially showed through. Sanderson and Bernard Heuvelmans, the scientist who gave cryptozoology its name, traveled to Minnesota. They wanted to examine the creature, known as the Minnesota Ice Man. The ice man's keeper, Frank Hansen, did not want the ice disturbed, but he was willing to have the two men examine it through the ice. Hansen told them that he had obtained the ice man in Hong Kong. (Many rumors went around about the creature's origin. Some said it had been shot in northern Wisconsin and then frozen; Sanderson believed it might have been found in Vietnam.)

The creature strongly resembled a sturdy human about six feet tall. Its legs were of normal length, although its feet were rather large. Its arms were longer than a human's and the hands were larger. Most scientists, if they showed any interest at all, thought the ice man was simply a sideshow gimmick. But Sanderson and Heuvelmans thought they had found something real—if not a Bigfoot, perhaps a Neanderthal man! What they could see of the creature's skin looked genuine. It had very distinct, individual hairs, as well as occasional pimples and lines and other characteristics of real skin. Sanderson and Heuvelmans thought it would be very hard to fake something this good.

Sanderson made detailed sketches and took a few photographs. Then he told scientists at the Smithsonian Institution in Washington, D.C., about this very interesting specimen. The scientists showed interest in examining the creature. But before they had a chance, it disappeared!

Hansen said the owner had come and taken it away. Three different organizations claimed they had made the creature, but Sanderson and Heuvelmans were still convinced that what they saw had a chance to be the real thing. Did Bigfoot live for a time in a block of ice at the Minnesota State Fair?

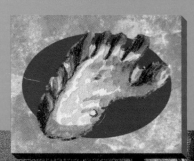

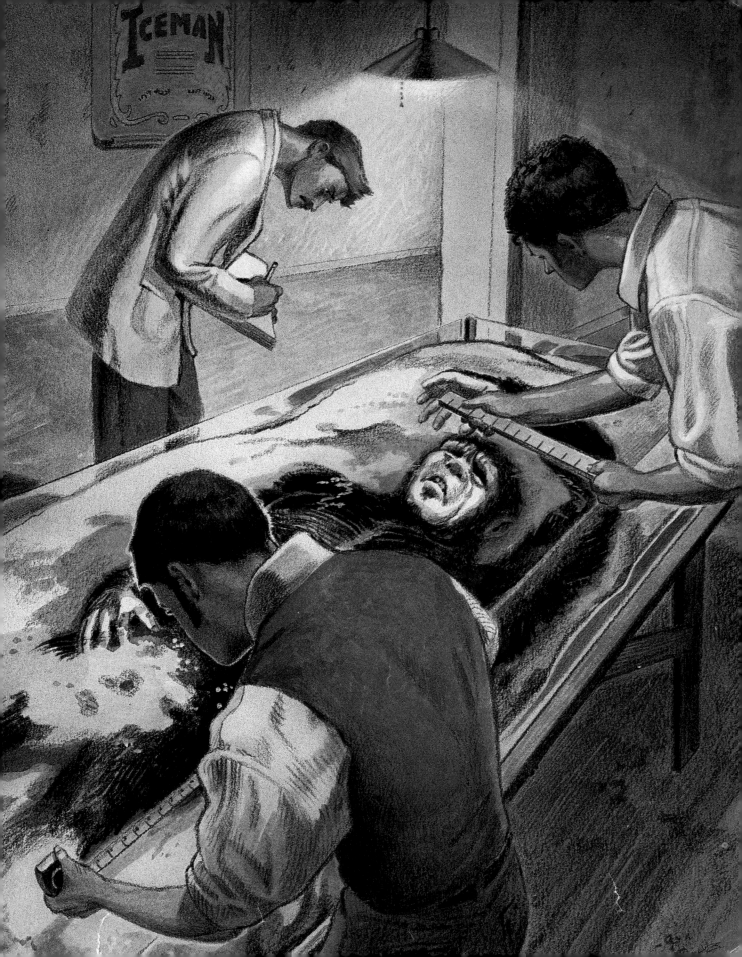

Biologist Stephen Jay Gould disagrees with Krantz's idea that scientists simply do not want to find out that Bigfoot is real. "Every natural historian would be delighted if this existed," he says. "We all root for these things."

Yet Gould is not ready to believe Krantz's evidence. "It just doesn't seem likely," he says. Even Krantz, convinced as he is, would like more proof. Like other Bigfoot hunters, he hopes for a piece of evidence that will prove beyond doubt that Bigfoot exists.

CHAPTER 3

The Story Continues

In 1967, Roger Patterson, a rodeo cowboy, thought he had the evidence everyone was looking for. Patterson filmed a Bigfoot!

Patterson had long been interested in Bigfoot, and he had been searching for the creature off and on for about six years. With his partner, Bob Gimlin, Patterson rode into a remote area of California on horseback. He was hoping to find evidence that Bigfoot existed. About twenty-five miles into rugged mountain country, the two men came around a bend in a creek, and their horses suddenly reared. On the other side of the creek, about eighty to a hundred feet away, stood a large, hairy creature.

Patterson's horse threw him. He struggled to his feet and then ran after the creature. As he ran, he operated a movie camera he had brought with him. When he got closer to the creature, it turned and looked at him. He said, "It looked at me with such an expression of . . . disgust, that I just stayed right there." He stopped running and continued to film. Gimlin was so stunned, he just sat on his horse, rifle in hand, and did nothing but watch.

The film Patterson took shows what appears to be a female Bigfoot walking along a stream bed. At first the film jumps about, because Patterson could not keep the camera steady while he was running. When the film settles down, the Bigfoot can be seen swinging her arms as she walks. She turns to look at the camera, then she disappears into the woods.

Several days later, Bob Titmus, a Bigfoot investigator, studied the tracks left in the area. He reconstructed the scene. He concluded that the Bigfoot had been only twenty-five feet away when it and the men first sighted each other.

The film was big news. Patterson showed it to many scientists, but most of them considered it a hoax. Patterson wanted to convince them that his film was not a fake. So he took it to the Disney movie studios and asked the special effects people if they could create a creature that would look and move like the creature in his film. They studied the film and said that it would be almost impossible.

René Dahinden believed the film was real. He took it to experts in Europe, including an anatomist named Dr. Don Grieve who specializes in human movement. Grieve said that if the film was taken at normal speed, the creature's movements were not like those of a human or of any animal he knew. Unfortunately, Patterson did not know what speed his camera had been set on.

These experts could not agree whether Patterson's film showed a real Bigfoot or not. If it was a hoax, they said, it was one of the best hoaxes ever concocted. But the scientists told Dahinden they could not be sure the creature in the film was real.

(Left) Anthropologist Grover Krantz with a cast of the footprint taken after a Sasquatch sighting near Walla Walla, Washington. Roger Patterson's film of Bigfoot in 1967 is still the most convincing proof of the beast's existence. (Clockwise, left) A cast of the foot of the creature in the film shows its size relative to an adult male's; Roger Patterson (right) and Bob Gimlin examine track casts left by the film creature; a slide from the film shows Bigfoot running away from Patterson.

The Walla Walla Prints

Dahinden and others were disappointed that the film still did not prove Bigfoot's existence. Over the next several years, searchers found and examined many footprints. Authorities checked many reports of sightings. But nothing conclusive turned up—until 1982.

That year, a Forest Service patrol officer found fifteen-inch-long footprints in the forest near Walla Walla, Washington. Many footprints had been found before, but these were different. The prints had been made in soil so fine that dermal ridges could be seen. Der-

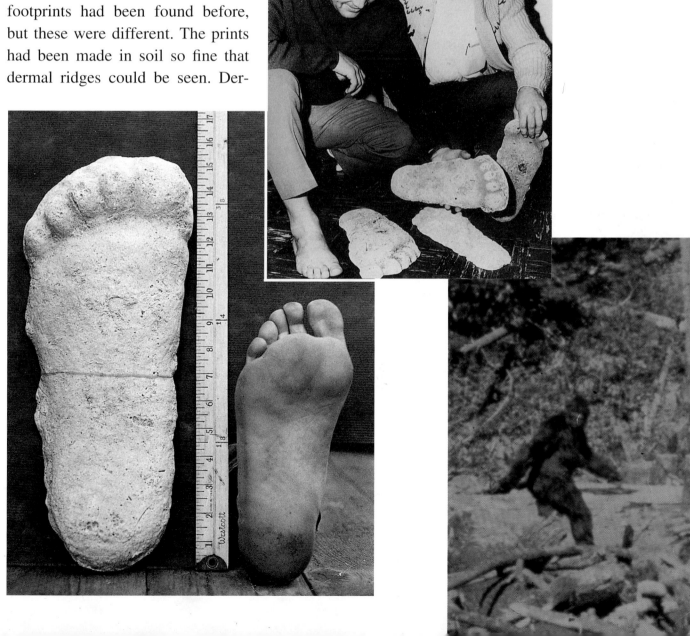

Does Bigfoot Come from Outer Space?

Some people believe Bigfoot comes from outer space. In their book *Bigfoot*, authors B. Ann Slate and Alan R. Berry tell of an incident that happened in Pennsylvania in 1973. Several people saw a glowing ball come down from the sky and land on the grass. Fifteen of these people were fascinated enough to gather on a nearby hilltop to see what was happening. The glowing object—a UFO, or unidentified flying object—made a noise something like a lawnmower as it descended. The people saw two tall, hairy monsters step out of the UFO. The creatures had shining yellow-green eyes. (Many people who have seen a Bigfoot at night have reported that it has glowing yellow or green eyes, much like those of a night animal caught in headlights).

A man in the crowd shot at one of the creatures with his rifle. The creature made a whining noise, and at that instant, the UFO vanished. A faint, low-lying light lingered at the landing site for a time, but no sign was found of the two creatures.

There have been other reports that connect Bigfoot with UFOs. In one incident, also in Pennsylvania, but in 1966, some people claimed they encountered a Bigfoot face-to-face. First they saw strange lights in the sky, then a Bigfoot-type creature approached their car, which was stuck in the mud. The creature scratched the sides and roof of the car before going away. The next day, investigating police officers claimed they found signs of a UFO and of tracks going from the UFO landing site to the place where the car had been stuck.

mal ridges are the little lines like fingerprints that are found on the soles of human and ape feet. The officer made careful casts of the prints.

The find delighted Grover Krantz. He showed the casts to several fingerprint experts. They had no doubts the prints were real. They were not the prints of a human.

But could someone fake dermal ridges? Krantz decided to find out. He asked a colleague to make a fake cast with dermal ridges. Then he showed it to the experts who had examined the cast from the forest. They knew immediately that it was a fake. But Walter Birkby was still not convinced the Walla Walla cast was real. Birkby was a forensic anthropologist (a person who studies human beings for the legal system) at the University of Arizona. "I need something that can't be faked before I run out and buy a big block of Sasquatch stock," he said. "Give me a skull and some dentition [teeth]."

Apparently skeptics would not be convinced. Bigfoot hunters waited for more evidence, as sightings of Bigfoot continued.

A Bigfoot peers out from the forest as a surprised oil crew member points him out.

An Important Sasquatch Sighting

In March 1987, an oil crew in British Columbia reported a Bigfoot sighting. Seven men were working outdoors when four of them saw something near their work site. The creature bent down and watched the men through the trees for a while. Then it moved away.

The men agreed that the creature was about seven feet tall and weighed about four hundred pounds. Myles Jack, one of the workers, said it was "more like a man than an animal. But it was a real mover. It was really fluid in the way it moved."

Bryan Mestdagh, another worker, had turned to look at the creature when Jack called to him. "I've seen a documentary on the Sasquatch," said Mestdagh, "and I'd have to say what we saw was identical."

René Dahinden was called in to investigate. He noticed one print that looked as if the creature had been crouching, just as the workers had said. Dahinden was sure the footprints could not have been faked. Also, he noted that all four of the men told similar stories.

Ann Rees, a reporter for a newspaper in British Columbia, visited the isolated clearing, too. She wrote, "It's being dubbed the best Sasquatch sighting in almost a decade."

Hunting for Bigfoot in Ohio

As people become more eager to prove that Bigfoot exists, they are going into the woods after it rather than waiting to happen on one by chance. Bob Gardiner did that in 1989. He organized an expedition to find a live Bigfoot in Vinton County, Ohio, in the Experimental Forest near the town of MacArthur.

Most people think of Bigfoot as roaming the woods of the Pacific Northwest, yet several Bigfoot sightings are reported in Ohio every year. Most people are sure that more than one of these creatures inhabit the Experimental Forest.

Bob Gardiner has searched for Bigfoot for more than twenty years. On this particular expedition, he wanted to test a theory. He believes Bigfoot is more curious about women than men, so he included several women in his search party. "More girls and kids have spotted it than men," Gardiner explains.

Before nightfall, the group found prints in the mud of a creek near their camp. The prints revealed toelike impressions and appeared to be not more than twelve hours old. Several times during the night the campers heard noises in the woods, but they could not tell what the noises were.

Gardiner's plan was for most of the group to stay in camp to attract the attention of a curious Bigfoot. A few others would hide in the underbrush waiting to see it. Unfortunately, the local press caught wind of Gardiner's search party. Reporters and television camera crews flooded the area with light. They tramped around the search party's camp and interviewed the members. A carload of spectators drove by hooting their version of a Bigfoot mating call. If a Bigfoot was in the Experimental Forest, it stayed away from Gardiner and his group.

What Will Convince Science?

Stories of Bigfoot sightings in North America have been around for several centuries. But until the 1950s, the idea of Bigfoot was pretty well limited to two groups: those few people who thought they saw the creature, and Native American tribes, who had a tradition of belief in a Bigfoot kind of creature. Bigfoot did not hit the news in a big way until Jerry Crew gave it its popular name—Bigfoot—in 1958.

Many of the sighting reports are based solely on the words of the witnesses. But many others have some kind of evidence to back them up. The most common evidence is footprints—the experts have casts of more than two thousand of them. But a few people have also found handprints, bits of Bigfoot fur, and teeth marks. And of course, scientists have Roger Patterson's film. Many of these bits of evidence are unexplained. Scientific study has not been able to prove them fakes. Why, then, do most scientists still refuse to believe that Bigfoot is real?

Body Needed

Grover Krantz says, "in the eyes of science, no animal exists until it is proven beyond any possibility of doubt." He says that only one kind of evidence has a chance of convincing scientists. That evidence is a specimen—a Bigfoot, whether alive or dead—or a very large part of one.

Some Bigfoot hunters have tried using high-tech equipment. They have used thermal detectors, night-vision instruments, and infrared imagers. These special pieces of equipment have helped hunters and scientists track wolf packs, see human enemies in the dark, and distinguish the shape of their prey in a deep, dark forest. But none of them has found Bigfoot.

Not even the dead body of a Sasquatch has ever been found. This is one thing many scientists point to when they say that Bigfoot cannot be real. But some experts think that Bigfoots bury their dead, just as certain other kinds of wild animals do. They also point out that dead bodies in the damp, cool environment of northern forests would decompose and disappear fairly quickly. Large numbers of animal, bird, and insect scavengers would aid this process.

Krantz points out that there are probably a hundred bears for every Sasquatch in a given territory, and bodies of bears that aren't killed by humans are almost never found. Ivan Sanderson was a naturalist and cryptozoologist. He wrote:

> Ask any game warden, real woodsman, or professional animal collector if he has ever found the dead body or even a bone of any wild animal—except along roads, of course, or if killed by man. I never have, in 40 years on five continents! Nature takes care of its own, and damned fast, too.

Why then should we expect to find a Bigfoot body?

Dead or Alive?

But just suppose that someone could figure out a way to find a Bigfoot. What should he or she do then? Scientists, hunters, and others argue about this. Some think the best thing would be to shoot the Bigfoot. That way, science would have a specimen to study. Others say this would be a terrible, inhuman thing to do; the best thing would be to capture it—perhaps by shooting it with a tranquilizer dart.

Grover Krantz thinks the very best thing would be to find a Bigfoot that has died a natural death. That way scientists could study its skin, its blood, its skeleton, and its organs. There would be no question that Bigfoots exist, and scientists would be able to discover much about the creature.

But, he points out, this is a very difficult task. In his book

Big Footprints, he suggests that the best time to try is probably winter. That is when "old age, disease, tooth loss, or other infirmities would weaken them too much to get through this difficult season." In the northwest, where many Sasquatches are reported, a dead Bigfoot's body would quickly freeze and would be preserved for a time. He thinks that if Bigfoot

The northwestern United States and Canada is Bigfoot country. Here, dense forests and high, snow-covered mountains make many areas inaccessible to humans.

hunters could survey people who live in likely areas, they could find some kind of pattern in the places animal remains are found. They might be able to find out the kinds of places large animals, such as bears, go to die. Then they could keep a watch on such areas, in the hopes of finding a dead Bigfoot.

An Elusive Creature

If Bigfoot does exist in Ohio, or California, or anywhere in North America, it seems to want to keep to itself. It is seen only when humans venture into remote areas, and then usually at night and only for fleeting moments.

Many of the people who have reported seeing a Bigfoot are reliable, sensible people not known for lying or playing practical jokes. But, asks biologist Stephen Jay Gould, "If [Bigfoot] exists, Why is it that all we have are fuzzy photographs and footprints?" Why has a Bigfoot never been captured, or the remains of a Bigfoot been found?

Peter Byrne is an author and dedicated Bigfoot hunter. He thinks perhaps the Sasquatches bury their dead the way humans do. He tells of a man who swore he watched three Bigfoots burying a fourth. But if Byrne is right, why has no one found fossils of Bigfoot bones? Byrne has an explanation for that, too. He says that in the wet, acidic soil of the Pacific Northwest, bones disappear without fossilizing.

Richard Beeson, a scientist at the University of Idaho, thinks the reason is simple: Even the honest people have imagined Bigfoot. They have heard stories, then seen strange shapes in the shadows of the woods. Their imaginations take over, and they think they're seeing a Bigfoot.

But Dr. Myra Shackley, a university professor, disagrees. There is enough reliable information, she believes, to think that there must be something to the stories. Even some universities now sponsor Bigfoot research, which they would not do if they thought Bigfoot was just a myth.

When will someone prove that Bigfoot is real? Maybe

never. Construction crews are building more and more roads in the U.S. and Canadian wilderness. Many experts are afraid that more traffic and houses will frighten these strange creatures. They are afraid the Bigfoots will have no room to live and will become extinct before anyone can prove they exist.

But some people hope that Bigfoot is never caught. "Wilderness," according to one writer, "is a mystery, a not knowing. . . . Let its mysteries remain, so we'll always have a wilderness to keep a mystery like Bigfoot . . . alive."

Glossary

anatomy: Having to do with the parts of the body.

anthropologist: A person who studies people's origins and cultures.

biology: The study of plant and animal life.

catalog: A complete list of items, with descriptions.

colleague: A person in the same profession.

cryptozoology: The study of unseen animals.

elusive: Hard to capture or see.

expedition: A journey undertaken for a certain purpose.

folklore: The customs, stories, and sayings of a group of people.

geographer: A person who studies the land and oceans of the earth.

hoax: A trick intended to fool people.

mountaineer: A person who climbs mountains for sport.

primate: A human, ape, or monkey.

prospecting: To look for valuable minerals, especially gold.

snuff: Tobacco that is chewed and placed between the cheek and gums or breathed in through the nose.

spectator: A person who watches.

supervisor: A person who is in charge of other workers.

survey: To look over and measure something.

terrain: The physical features of an area of land.

tranquilizer: A drug that makes an animal or person sleepy.

zoologist: A person who studies animals.

For Further Reading

Mary Calhoun, *The Night the Monster Came.* New York: Morrow, 1982.

Mary Blount Christian, *The Mystery of Bigfoot.* Mankato, MN: Crestwood House, 1987.

Hal G. Evarts, *Bigfoot.* New York: Scribner, 1973.

Michael Grumley, *There Are Giants in the Earth.* Garden City, NY: Doubleday, 1974.

Jamie James, "Bigfoot or Bust," *Discover*, March 1988.

Robert Franklin Leslie, *Ringo, the Robber Raccoon: The True Story of a Northwoods Rogue.* New York: Dodd, Mead, 1984.

Ruth Shannon Odor, *Bigfoot.* Mankato, MN: Child's World, 1989.

Marian T. Place, *Bigfoot All Over the Country.* New York: Dodd, Mead, 1978.

Marian T. Place, *Nobody Meets Bigfoot.* New York: Dodd, Mead, 1976.

Marian T. Place, *On the Track of Bigfoot.* New York: Dodd, Mead, 1974.

Gardner Soule, *The Maybe Monsters.* New York: Putnam, 1963.

Works Consulted

Norma Gaffron, *Bigfoot*. San Diego: Greenhaven Press, 1989.

John Napier, *Bigfoot: The Yeti and Sasquatch in Myth and Reality*.

John Ellis Sech, "A Search for Bigfoot," *Fate*, January 1990.

Mike Wyatt, "The Bigfoot Primer," *Backpacker*, August 1990.

Index

About the Author

Julie S. Bach is a writer and editor who lives in St. Paul, Minnesota. Among her writings is a biography for young people, *Diana, Princess of Wales*. Bach enjoys camping with her husband and their dogs. She and her husband plan to take a vacation in the Pacific Northwest someday. If they meet Bigfoot face to face, they hope they'll remember to use their cameras.

Picture Credits